# CONTAINER
# GARDENING
## FOR BEGINNERS

# TABLE OF CONTENTS

# INTRODUCTION

Thank you for choosing *Container Gardening for Beginners: The Ultimate Guide to Growing Vegetables, Herbs, Fruits, and Edibles Flowers in Tubs, Pots, and Other Containers.*

Did you know that without large spaces for traditional gardening you can grow fruits and vegetables in containers in your garden? Almost every vegetable and plant that grows in a garden will also thrive in containers. Ranging from vegetables such as lettuce, tomatoes, peppers, radishes, eggplants and carrots, fruit like peaches, apples, blueberries, Meyer melons, and bananas, herbs such as sage, thyme, basil, chives and parsley, and even edible flowers like roses, violets, begonia pansies and calendula. Generally, solid crops such as bush beans also grow well in pots and look perfect when placed with other plants in containers.

This guide provides you with remarkable information on the most straightforward and best ways to grow the good food we eat, choosing the best plants in pots, picking the right pot size for plants, a technique to keeping your plants healthy, controlling pests and plant diseases and much more!

# CHAPTER ONE

## Why Container Gardening

- **Good Family Bonding**

Since container gardening makes the gardening process simpler, don't be surprised that your children love it. Bearing this in mind, container gardening can be a perfect way of bonding as a family. While you get to enjoy the quality time and share knowledge, your kids also enjoy healthy veggies and growing success.

- **Saves Water**

You need lots of water when you water a garden as a whole. Whether you working with a shortage of water supplies, or you are preserving water for other domestic uses, gardening with container is an excellent choice.

- **Sunlight isn't a Problem**

If your yard has a lot of shady areas that make growing a traditional garden difficult, you will enjoy container gardening as you have the liberty of moving your garden around as necessary to meet the sun. If lack of sunlight was your issue with gardening, container gardening has given you a new option.

- **Fewer Pest Issues**

Container gardens can be easily moved around. This makes it difficult for diseases and pests to survive, which amount to your garden's safety. You would be spending lesser amount of time combating pests trying to destroy your garden. Thus you enjoy gardening more.

- **Produces Healthy Plants**

Container gardening makes gardening much easier by creating more suitable atmosphere for plants to strive with fewer pests than a large garden. Consequently, it produces healthier plants.

- **Convenience**

Lastly, gardening in containers is convenient in term of planting, caring for your plants and harvesting your bounty.

# CHAPTER TWO

## Planning Your Gardening

Container Gardening which is also known as Urban Gardening is an excellent means of adding spices, veggies, and life to your living space. You could allow plant containers to grow in the interior of your house in a semi-sunny, windowsill spot, outdoor on a walkway or deck. Your only limitation is the type of plants you intend to grow and space. You may plan to grow flowers and plants for dramatic impact or color, or herbs and veggies for your table, or a mixture of both ornamental and edible crops. The choice is yours.

Firstly, you need to consider the space where you will place your containers. A patio or sunny deck is an ideal space to begin, however, numerous plants will grow well on a ledge or shelf. If you have a broad passageway, it would be perfect. However, the following are the things to put into consideration when planning your garden:

## 1. **Space:**

You can draw a plan of your environment that would show your containers. Take note of the direction of sunlight and the amount of sun receive on a daily basis in your area. Give room for about two times diameter of the pot or container for minimum space between them.

## 2. **Time**:

You also need to put in plan the amount of time to be spent in your garden per week. Whether you grow flowers or vegetables, you will be required to water them many times a week. They would also need to be pruned, weeded, fertilized, and picked over and more. Therefore, be practical about the amount of time you will be spending in your garden.

## 3. Expenses:

You can use virtually anything as a gardening container. You need to dig holes in some buckets or pots to give room for adequate drainage. Plants could add up in quantity, in particular, if you buy trees or shrubs in large quantity for your container. Buying soil and amendments could be expensive especially if you have several pots to fill.

## 4. Seeds or plants:

You can begin your gardening with seeds for a variety of vegetables, herbs, and flowers. This is a wonderful and economical way to start. However, you can as well plant large flower shrubs in big galvanized buckets or trees in half whiskey containers.

**HERE ARE SOME VALUABLE TIPS:**

- Make use of five-gallon plastic buckets, you can get this from a few restaurants or buy at a local large box store. Vegetables grow perfectly well in them because there is enough room for the root to grow. If you feel like changing their color, you can paint them with plastic surface paint.

- You can look for available containers that you can make use of within your premises, in particular for a smaller windowsill garden. If your interest is limited to merely small plants such as herbs, indoor flowers, you can use teapots, coffee mugs, canisters, pencil holders and the likes for planting. What is most important for plants is spacing, give your plants enough space for roots to develop so as to give them chance to grow well.

- There also available a variety of DIY kits for container gardens, though the majority of them are designed for vegetables but, suitable for other variety of plants.

- After you have determined your timing, space, and budget and have an overall idea of the kind of plants to cultivate, the next thing is to conclude on the varieties that are good for you.

- The exciting thing about growing your own vegetables or flowers is that you can decide to choose exotic varieties (the types that are not available at a grocery store or nursery).

- Where do you find plants suitable for containers? Though many garden centers and larger box stores only sell specific container plants, there are a whole lot of varieties available elsewhere.

- You can find a lot of beautiful and latest choices via seed catalogs. Try to get an array of options with determinate growth (those plants with specific end) they grow to a particular level and stop, different from plants that grow indefinitely. Mostly, they do not need to be upheld with a trellis or stick to grow up. They also add additional energy from their plants into fruits and flowers rather than developing long vines. Beans, squash, cucumbers, and tomatoes all fall in determinate and indeterminate (develop into long vines).

- Although many bigger box stores and garden centers do carry container-specific plants, there is a whole world of choices.

- Many seed companies give their catalogs for free, and they present a wealth of information. The suitable varieties for containers will be marked or even in their own segment. Most will carry growing instructions, photos, space, and sunlight requirements.

- They can assist you to set up your garden environment even if you do not purchase your plants and seeds directly from the catalog.

- Most of the seed companies have advanced into gardening companies, and give more than just seeds. Plants can be bought and be shipped at the right time for you to plants in your container.

- Some of their root may be exposed and look as if they are dead, but do not worry they are still very alive. They will flourish when cultivated.

- You can purchase trees and shrubs via the mail, as well as houseplants, cacti, herbs, and succulents.

- If you are to buy plants via mail, ensure they are from a trustworthy and certified seller that can send plants to your state. There are applicable limitations to the state to state shipments because of soil diseases and contaminants.

- If you intend on growing flowers, most floral plants do not require similar spacing as vegetable plants. Since they have a more extensive root system and need more nutrients and bigger containers

- Once you've decided on what plants you plan to cultivate, you can contact your local garden store for them to advise on the varieties that will grow perfectly well in your location, and there is every possibility they will have them in store.

# CHAPTER THREE

## Garden Tools and Accessories

Gardening can be done in several ways, but if you have chosen a container garden you should have certain gardening tools for you to succeed. If you intend to acquire the most substantial part of your crops, you need to begin the planning before time. Purchase your seeds and garden equipment so that there will be time to sprout and germinate seeds.

Numerous gardening tools could be purchased, but the following are the most essential tools for container gardening:

1. **Small shovel**:

A small shovel is perfect for pots. It makes it simple to dig in fertilizers and also to plant your crops or seeds in the pot.

### 2. **Hand Weeder**:

A hand weeder is a small fork class of tool with a long neck. It's useful for planting seeds and small plants and removing the little weeds that grow in containers. It can be used to dig a tiny hole to put the plant or seed in.

### 3. **Plant containers**:

A plant container is a container for the crops and it has to be the right size. You can make use of any type of container for growing plants and vegetable crops. Wooded boxes or crates, gallon-sized coffee cans, old washtubs, as well as five-gallon buckets can be used for growing vegetables in as much as there is sufficient drainage.

### 4. **Small cups or egg Cartons to start seeds**.

You can use this for sprouting seeds. Ascertain your container is sufficiently broad to give room for the seeds to germinate. If you do not have enough space, the plants have to be transplanted as they grow. Also, you may need to buy a seed heating device as most times you a required to sprout them within, for it to be adequately warm so that they can germinate and grow.

### 5. **Soil**:

Quality potting soil is a determinant for your plants to grow well. It is the secret to a successful container garden. If you use poor soil, your plants or seeds will not grow. The soil means a lot. Make sure you get top quality soil that your plants require to thrive with or without fertilizer.

6. **Plant seeds**:

A plant seed can be flower or vegetable seeds. The ideal thing is to look for high-quality seeds if you are to plant vegetables to be able to harvest seeds and keep for another season. Determinate tomatoes and shrub type plants grow brilliantly well in containers. If you're looking forward to the best crops in your pots, go for these types of plants.

7. **Garden Gloves**:

Though garden glove may not be very essential if you are the type that easily got disgusted by dirt and doesn't want stain beneath your nails, or sensitive to some particular plants, you need garden gloves. Also if you do not want to lay your hand on a caterpillar, tomato hornworm, snail and gardens insects when removing them from your favorite crops, garden gloves do the job better. It will also guard your hands against thorns or all other sharp component of the plants.

8. **Watering can**:

Watering can do the job better by making the task of watering plants simple and trouble-free because water is running out of it in form of trickling rain. You can, however, make use of a milk jug to convey water outside. But if you are to use it, ensure you gently pour the water in your hand and spread with your fingers to enable the water to scatter and drop softly into the soil. If not, water coming from jug may land heavily on the soil and splash back on the crop's foliage, raising its danger of having fungus issues and other infections.

## 9. **Trowel**:

A trowel is also an essential tool for container gardening, it is being used to loosen up compressed dirt as well as digging through trash in plant containers. Rather than using your hands, the trowel will get the task done better and faster and leave your hand dirt free.

## 10. **Pruners**

This is useful for cutting off dead foliage and pruning plants. Though you might think of using scissors, it is not advisable to use it. There are wet saps on plants which may leave remains stick and rust on your scissors. Cutting plants with scissors instead of pruner also increase the risk of the plants being infected. Pruner is more active in cutting thicker crop stems, also enable clean cut while leaving your plants healthier in the containers.

## 11. **Plant Organic Pesticide**

If you are a non-fastidious type who could squish insects and not have a bad feeling, a pesticide may not be necessary for you. However, if the reverse is the case, it is ideal you have a plant-safe pesticide as part of your tools. Ensure you adhere to all instructions on its usage because it may not be good on food plants. Possibly, you can remove the pest from the plants and spray on the floor with the pesticide.

## 12. Stick or String

These are essential for supporting container plants that needed to be upheld. An example is tomato plants (string and stick or tomato cage can be used to support tomatoes). They can also be used for young trees that needed to be upheld to grow in a straight line up and plants growing up the fence. Stick can be bought at your local garden store. String or yarn could be an organic color, like brown or dark green for it not to stand out in the garden environment.

## 13. Quality Fertilizer

Fertilizer is also essential for the growth of your plant. Having secured good soil, ensure you obtain a high-quality organic fertilizer to get the best result from crops. Fertilizer can be in pellet or liquid form.

You can buy specific fertilizer for each type of your plants like rose or citrus fertilizer. However, an all-purpose plant fertilizer does the job for most gardeners. Compost can as well be used to supplement your crop's feeding

### 14. **Potting Bench**:

A potting bench is also an essential tool for gardeners. Firstly it serves as a platform to assemble and store your small appliances, plant marker, fertilizer and the likes. You can also use it to conveniently move your planting tools from one place to another (for example, from your kitchen to your garden)

Each of the gardening tools is very important for your container garden to be successful. Make sure have them at your disposal to ease work as well as

getting the best results out of your products.

# CHAPTER FOUR

## Selecting Pots for Plants

Be creative when picking pots for plants. Like I've said earlier, you can use any material for pot in as much as it does not get too hot under the sun and drains well. If your choosing pots are not having sufficient drainage holes, ensure you make a few good sized holes on them. If you cannot drill holes on a particular planter, it can be however worked around by planting in a different pot and situate it in your preferred container.

You also need to put the size of the plants you would be growing into consideration when choosing a container. If you choose a smaller pot, the soil may not be able to obtain sufficient moisture, in no time plants will turn out to be root bound and dry out, hence leading to plant destruction. Then again, if your container is vast, your crops might use up all their energy on developing root and not sufficiently on growth. The West Virginia University Extension Service stated that shallow-rooted plants such as herbs, peppers, lettuce and most annuals require a planter of no less than six-inch in diameter with eight-inch soil depth. Bigger containers such as ½ whiskey barrels and bushel basket are suitable for growing pole beans, cucumbers, tomatoes, and most perennial crops.

Planters and pots are available in many diverse shapes, sizes, and materials. Whichever type of container you choose, take the area where it would be utilized into consideration and plan accordingly. Select containers in appropriate quantity to the size of the plant.

### 1. **Terra-Cotta**

Terra-Cotta is available in different sizes and shapes, the pots look great with their plain color that brings out the beauty of nearly any plant. The product of porous soil rich in iron, it has breathing ability which keeps potting soils calm and drains surplus dampness out of the plant roots to maintain their health status. The major issues with terra-cotta are that it can quickly dry out particularly in hot climate and quite fragile (can be easily broken). Some growers choose glazed terra-cotta pots as they obtain water a lot better.

## 2. **Plastic**

If you don't care about having plants that ultimately grow to cover their pots or the look of the container, plastic is a better option. Plastics pots hold moisture well, durable and are reasonably cheap. They are also not heavy, which makes reorganizing your gardens an easy task. If your container garden is situated in an extremely sunny area, you are advised not to use a dark colored or black plastic. As they quickly get hot and also absorb heat which can cause roots damage. Bright colored container reflects the warmth and maintains the coolness in the roots.

## 3. **Wood**

Wood is among the most original and handy containers for gardening. They look good, not heaving and hold water well. If you are to choose wood containers, ensure they are made out of wood that is resistant to rotting such as redwood or cedar and confirm the construction quality since wood will naturally expand and shrink in the elements. Containers made out of soft-wood or pine can be as well used but has to be painted with a harmless paint to avoid rot. Wooden containers can be easily made with some scrap wood and some creative idea without stress.

4. **Concrete**

Concrete is ideal for holding large plants that need more support to keep them healthy due to its heaviness. It possesses excellent insulating materials, protecting tender roots systems by keeping a calm soil atmosphere. With a concrete container, you can leave your plants outdoor over the winter with no fear of harm (or even if you're planting in public area) since it has an additional advantage of preventing people from inadvertently working off with your valued pots or plants.

# CHAPTER FIVE

## What Plants Need To Flourish

After you must have decided on what you want, take into consideration what you can supply the plants given your area, space and time dedication. Plants require food, water, air, and light, but the quantity and quality different from plant to plant. Read plant descriptions on seed packets and cultivate plants with the same requirements together.

1. **Space**

Find out how huge a plant would be when fully-grown and ensure your container can contain it.

Small varieties usually grow well in pots due to their natural size.

## 2. **Potting Mix**

Plants in container thrive in a potting mix than in garden soil that could easily compact. More frequent, garden soil accommodates pests, weed seeds and other critters that are dangerous to your containers. Try to find a mix that is fluffy, light, drains well and have sufficient organic substance to retain nutrients and water. Pre-mixed potting soil can be purchased or you can prepare it by yourself. Ensure you read the package cautiously when buying potting soil. Spend your money on high-quality organic potting mix, instead of purchasing what is named as "compost or topsoil" which can be prepared from out of anything. If you decide to prepare your own, look for a good recipe and experiment. A typical soil-based mixture is:

- One part topsoil or garden loam

- One part matured compost or peat moss

- One clean perlite or builder sand

3. **Water**

Watering plants directly in the garden soil is entirely different from watering plants in containers. The soil in pots or containers is mostly dense than garden soil and as a result, keeps less water.

Moreover, the container limits the amount of soil to obtain water. And coupled with the fact that pots are over the ground, they do not have all it takes to maintain coolness. Inadequate or excess water can kill your plants. It's imperative to keep the soil moist all through, but not too damp. Most containers matured plants are required to be watered one time or two times per day in hot weather Make use of a watering can or garden hose to water the soil directly, when the water is sufficient, you can get digital moisture measuring device for accurate measurement,

If you are to be away from home for more than a few days, you can apply drip irrigation system to keep your plant alive. Make your own or purchase one. Water can also be retained for a long period by adding agro-polymers to the potting mixture or soil before planting.

4. **Mulch**

Your container will keep hold of their moisture on warm days and add nutrients to the soil when organic mulch is added to their top. Note, the nutrients leak out each time you watered and it's required to be replaced.

5. **Sunlight**

Most plants require six to eight hours of sunlight per day particularly vegetables, herbs, and fruits. If you do not experience that in your area, opt for varieties that grow well under shade like chard and spinach. Read seed packages to ascertain the sum of sunlight a particular variety need to flourish.

The package terms mean:

- Full sun: Plants require about six to eight hours of direct sunlight daily

- Partial sun: Plant needs about four to six hours of sunlight daily, if possible in the morning and early afternoon.

- Shade: Plants require less than four hours of sunlight daily, with filtered light for the rest of the day.

You may need to supply your containers an additional sunlight-boost with plant grow light when they have been moved indoors for the winter. There is available light specifically designed to aid plant growth during the dark of winter.

6. **Temperature**

Plants thrive at about 55 and $75^0$ F temperatures. When it lacks the insulating earth around containers, plant roots become cooler and hotter more rapidly than the plants in the ground. Shift containers indoor before it chills. Provide shade when it becomes hotter, you can group pots together to shade one another.

7.    **Nutrients/ Fertilizers**:

Nutrients mixtures like worm teas made from worm casting, compost teas, fish emulsion, liquid organic fertilizers and kelp meal supply required nitrogen, potassium and phosphorous additionally to an organic compound and micronutrient. Instead of synthetic fertilizers, these natural fertilizers will not burn your plants and provide the needed micronutrients as well as numerous macronutrients, vitamins, minerals, and amino acids. Most discharge their nutrients gradually (an adequate watering gets them started) providing you with long-term healthy results.

# CHAPTER SIX

## The Best Plants in Containers

Here are some vegetables and fruits that grow well in containers. It ranges from citrus fruits and banana to cucumber, tomatoes and all other crops that could be planted in a bigger garden. The disparity is, they can be grown on the porch or deck or anywhere you have space since they will be in containers. These plants thrive in pots, so you don't have to be concerned about getting less than half tomatoes. If what you desire is big beefsteak tomato in a container, then you will get it.

Whether you have a large gardening space or not and you wish to cultivate your own plants/food, these are the best varieties for you to cultivate in your containers. Look at them, Make your choices and make your way to home-produced crops in your house all year round.

- **Tomatoes**:

It is not a big deal that tomatoes thrive in containers. At least, they do put them up for sale in those upsides down growing containers. If you want fresh tomatoes all year round, they can be easily grown in any container size, it all depends on the type of tomato you intend to grow. You may decide to use a larger container to hold the plant, and you can start with starter plants or seeds, any of it go. Put an enclosed to the exterior of the container for additional support as the plant gets taller.

- **Basil**

This can be grown inside or outside and it is nice when added to soup and other recipes. You can grow basil for your favorite meal, even if you do not have an overall herb garden. All you need is some fresh potting soil, a 6-inch planter, and the basil. Always remember that when watering basil, you must avoid wetting the stem and leave. The best way is to spread water directly on top of the soil. Basil also needs a bit of direct sunlight daily, thus if you intend to cultivate it inside, ensure you make use of containers that can be easily moved out during the sunny period of the day.

- **Zucchini and Summer Squash**:

Every type of squash thrives in pots, especially summer squash. It will, grow well in any container. Squash is a versatile and resilient plant. Therefore, if you wish to put in fresh squash to your meals take some containers and grow the seeds. Always remember that you would be required to harvest the squash frequently when it starts to grow, for the plants not to get bogged down. In a week, you ought to acquire about three squash when they have started growing. Make sure you remove them to give space for new growth.

- **Parsley**

This also thrives in containers. Therefore, if you wish to add fresh parsley to your meals, you can simply grow the herb on the porch or balcony. It is a great herb to grow in your garden. It flourishes in small containers but needs partial sunlight and soil must be kept moisten to get the desired results. Parsley thrives in temperatures of about forty to eighty degrees F which makes it great for winter gardens. Just keep in mind to take it inside at night for it not to get too cold.

- **Strawberries**:

The fruit grows well in containers in spite of being observed as plants that require vast space to flourish. It's among the best plants that grow in a pot and do well even indoors. You can cultivate your own strawberries all year round in a sunny area of your house, possibly beside the window. You can use plant grow light to grow it during winter. Select larger containers that will house them sufficiently and also ensure they are reaped as they start producing to give room for more products.

- **Radishes**

Radishes also grow well in container gardens and can add spice to your dishes. Longer white varieties flourish in paint buckets and the likes while the short red type of radishes grows well in any kind of available container. This is a suggested vegetable plant for beginners since they grow greatly well in pots. Situate the containers out on the patio or by window side for them to receive sunlight in the daytime and ensure watering them every other day.

- **Pineapple**:

This fruit can be grown any time of the year in your containers, even if you are not dwelling in a tropical area. Cut off the cap of a fresh pineapple together with a small part of the fruit. Soak the cap in water for about 24 hours and then plant in a gallon sized plastic container. Pineapple requires a certain percentage of sunlight, thus you may need to place the container in the sunny area of your yards like deck and balcony. Always remember to take plants indoors at night, if you are growing in the winter.

- **Cantaloupe**

This lovely melon can be grown in containers. You need to get larger containers to cultivate the amount that will be sufficient all through summer if you don't have garden space in your house. Varieties of cantaloupe can be cultivated in containers, do not allow their vines to spread out, support them with sticks. The best variety of cantaloupe for container gardening are the smaller plants that produce smaller melons as there is more space for them to thrive. However, larger varieties can also be grown in as much as they have proper supports and trellis for vines to lean on.

- **Oregano**

This herb is a popular variety for container gardening and thrives in any container. Growing oregano in containers helps to keep them under control and prevent their spreading. Try to make use of small pots and potting soil. The herb is very easy to cultivate and grow well with no hitches. Situate your oregano in a sunny area in the daytime then take inside at night, particularly if you are growing in the winter.

- **Rosemary**

You do not necessarily need to have a large garden space before you grow herbs. Rosemary is one the herbs that grow well in containers. Make use of potting soil with least of peat moss, but you will put sand beneath the pot to give room for drainage and the surface ought to be given a chance to dry out before watering but should not dry completely.

- **Peppers**

Pepper is another plant that grows considerably well in containers. Be it green, yellow or red pepper, without you having garden space, you will have them available all year round. All you need to do is selecting the right container size for each variety. Bigger peppers will require a five or ten-gallon pot for them to have enough space to flourish, while smaller varieties need at least two-gallon containers. They also require about eight hours of sunlight per day, for this reason; try to position the containers to direct sunlight. If you like, you could be taking them inside in the night and returning them in the morning for direct sunlight.

- **Chives**:

Chives are indeed among the most robust herbs you can plant. These herbs thrive in containers or even wherever else you want them cultivated. They are perennial plants that flourish year in year out. They can add spices to your dips, baked tomatoes and your soups. Chives can be moved indoors if you want a continuous harvest all through the year. However, they also require a little bit of sunlight in the daytime to grow well, try placing your container in an area where they access slight sunlight.

- **Bananas**

If you like to be eating fresh bananas and you do not reside in a tropical area. Short sized banana could be well grown in containers within your compound, even in winter periods. It's also a perennial fruit that grows year in year out. For planting banana, you need relatively larger containers with adequate holes to allow for proper drainage so as for your plants not to drown out. It grows perfectly well indoors during winter and outdoors, whether in the deck or balcony in the summer.

- **Spinach**

Spinach is another plant that thrives in containers. It requires an eight-inch container per plant. Always remember that spinach doesn't want excessive heat so avoid wilting of the leaves by preventing it from direct sunlight. Containers normally become warm in the summer period, thus situate them in the shady area of your garden. Spinach can also be grown indoors in the winter season, you need to keep it watered regularly to prevent it from being dry out by the internal heat.

- **Thyme**

Thyme also grows perfectly well in containers whether indoors or outside. If you decide to have an herb garden in containers by planting thyme with oregano, basil, and other herbs or you only wish to grow your thyme in a container. The best pot for this herb is clay since it prevents water from drying out. Thyme would not flourish if over-logged with water, so ensure your selected container has a sufficient drainage hole. It can be grown inside in the winter period and as well requires bit sunlight during summer.

- **Potatoes**

Potatoes are also one of the crops that grow perfectly well in containers. They can be grown all through the year. Potatoes are ideal in 5-gallon buckets which could be easily shifted from indoors to outdoors for sunlight. Ensure there are adequate holes in the base of the bucket prior to planting to avoid crops dampness.

- **Sage**

Sage is also an herb that thrives in containers whether indoors or outside. The herb requires sunlight, if you do not have adequate sunlight during the winter, it may need artificial lighting. If you intend to cultivate it either in your window box or balcony, try to situate the containers directly to sunlight for the plant to receive enough in the daytime. But if you are growing it indoors, supply it with adequate lighting during the day.

- **Cucumbers**

Cucumber is an easy to grow vegetable even in containers. It can be kept growing all year long, be it in summer or winter season. It can as well be grown vertically to make the most of your available space.

Just allow them vines up the side of your house or even your deck railing if the containers would be placed outdoors. Midget-pickets, space-masters, and salad bush hybrids are the finest cucumber varieties for container gardening. Though, other varieties also grow well if well catered for. Ensure you give enough space for the vines and harvest the grown cucumber in due time so as not to outweigh and weaken the vines.

- **Kale**

With little available space in your garden, you can conveniently grow kale in containers. About 5 kales could be grown in a twenty-inch pot, growing them in containers make them to be easily moved indoors and outside during winter and summer respectively. You can start your kale planting with either seeds or transplants any of it goes. Avoid excessive moisture and at the same time too much dryness, hence apply moderation while watering, to enable the plants to thrive.

- **Lettuce**:

This is also one of the best plants that thrive in containers. Its container could be placed on the deck or balcony for direct sunlight and you can start your seedling just before the end of winter period for another plant season. You only need to plant the seed directly using a bigger container with potting soil inside. Lettuce can be planted with other greens like arugula or cilantro if you wish to maximize space. It can also be transplanted into a bigger container when the plants started growing.

- **Quinoa**

This whole grain food is rich in nutrients and it makes a perfect plant for container gardening. Quinoa is a hardy plant that can be perfectly grown on patios, indoors or about anywhere in your garden. Seeds should be planted directly in bigger containers with potting mix inside. The containers must be about 2 feet tall to enhance their growth.

- **Collard Greens**

Collard green is another plant that thrives in containers as long as the containers are placed in the direct sunlight of about six hours in daytime all through the spring and fall season. If growing in summer, situate the containers from indoors to a little shady location in the daytime. However, they will require direct sunlight in the fall and spring season. Collard greens can be grown all year round but you may need to provide plant grow light if growing in the period of winter.

# CHAPTER SEVEN

# Choosing the Right Size Pot for Your Plant

Garden containers could be measured in either gallons or inches. (Inches means the distance across the top of the container or the pot diameter) The following guide will help you in picking the right size pot for each plant.

**Plant a ten-inch (two and a half to three gallons) pot with:**

- Leaf lettuce (one)

- Strawberry (one)

- Swiss chard (one)

- Bush beans (one)

- Small herbs, such as Parsley, Mint, Chives or Sage (one)

- Annuals (one to three)

- Turnips (four)

- French (round) carrots (eleven to twelve)

**Plant a fourteen-inch (six to seven gallon) pot with:**

- Collards (one)

- Cabbage (one)

- Larger herbs, such as Lavender or Rosemary (one)

- Edamame (two)

- Peas (four)

- Annuals (three to four)

- Arugula, Spinach or Leaf lettuce (three to four)

- Dwarf sweet corn (six to seven)

- Carrots (nine to ten)

**Plant a sixteen-inch (nine to ten gallon) pot with:**

- Dwarf citrus tree (one)

- Dwarf shrub (one)

- Gooseberry (one)

- Goji berry (one)

- Dwarf bush-type fruits, such as Blueberry or Raspberry (one)

- Pole beans on a trellis (three to four)

- Annuals (four to six)

**Plant an eighteen-inch (fourteen to fifty gallon) pot with:**

- Pepper (one)

- Eggplant (one)

- Cauliflower (one)

- Broccoli (one)

- Determinate (or bush) tomato and support (one)

- Multiple herbs (varies)

- Multiple annual flowers (varies)

- Any type of leafy vegetables, greens (varies; see seed packet or plant tag for spacing guidelines)

**Plant a twenty-four -inch (twenty-four to twenty-five gallon) pot with:**

- Cucumber (one)

- Pomegranate (one)

- Fig tree (one)

- Summer squash (one)

- Evergreen shrub (one)

- Columnar apple (one)

- Blackberry or raspberry (one)

- Dwarf nectarine or peach (one)

- Indeterminate (with vine) tomato and cage (one)

- Ornamental shrub, such as butterfly bush, shrub rose or hydrangea (one)

- Annuals in multiples

## Plant a thirty-inch (thirty gallons) pot with:

- Rhubarb (one)

- Sweet corn (one)

- Dwarf cherry tree (one)

- Pumpkin (one, bush varieties are best)

67

- Espalier fruit tree, such as plum, pear or apple (one)

## Good Container Flowers suitable for Sun:

- Tuberous Begonia

- Zinnia

- Dahlia

- Verbena

- Angelonia

- Lantana

- African daisy (Arctotis)

- Purple fountain grass

## Good Container Flowers suitable for Shade:

- Torenia

- Browallia

- Impatiens

- Fuchsia

## Good and Colorful Foliage Plants suitable for Shade and Sun:

- Ornamental grass (different types, full sun)

- Ornamental sweet potato vine (Ipomoea batatas,( part shade/ full sun)

- Persian shield (Strobilanthesdyerianus, (part shade/ full sun)

- Ferns (different types, (filtered sun to shade)

- Coleus (shade and sun, depending on variety)

- Canna (part shade to full sun)

- Phormium (part shade to full sun)

- Caladium (shade)


## Good Container Flowers for Sun and Shade

- Salvia (Salvia guarantica, part shade/full sun)

- Scaevola (part shade/full sun)

- Nemesia (part shade/full sun)

- Mini Petunia (Calibrachoa part shade/full sun)

- Twinspur (Diascia, part shade/full sun)

- Note: Where I listed on the name, the common names and the botanical are the same.

# CHAPTER EIGHT

## Controlling Pests and Plant Diseases

**Note**: The below tips are not meant only for container gardening, they're for gardening as a whole.

Container plants naturally experience fewer pest attacks since they are grown in a cleaner and more regularly sanitized environment than field or garden plants. Nevertheless, it does not make them free from pests, diseases or other issues. An insect could sneak into any garden, and fungal spores are always present in the air. "Plant diseases, weeds, and pests can be a danger to crops. The only solution is to spray pesticides regularly", says "chemical companies" However, chemicals might create more issues than they resolve. Sustainable farming aligns with nature to maintain soil, crops, weeds, diseases and pest life in balance. We call this integrated pest management (IMP) or natural pest management.

Integrated pest management prevents pest problems and plant diseases, and keeps unsafe chemicals away from us and our surroundings. It as well prevents problems of pesticides resistance and chemical reliance. Even though you are to make use of pesticides, it is significant to ascertain if pests are damaging your plants, the intensity of the damage being done, and whether creatures in the garden are already taken care of the pest. After that, you can take a decision on if and when chemicals are to be used, and what type to use. The best method to control both diseases and pests is to ensure plants remain healthy.

## Start with Prevention

- Select disease-resistant types. Numerous vegetables and ornamental plants have been confirmed to be resistant to diseases, like rust, mildew, and canker.

- Examine plants before buying them to ascertain they're healthy. After that, carefully clean them prior to planting.

- Do not over-crowd your plants. Ventilation prevents the condition of dampness that encourages the growth of fungi and other diseases.

- Take note of moisture levels. If the soil is too dry or too wet to correct the situations. Ensure plants dryness all the time.

- Examine your plants. Attend to issues before getting out of hand. Take out and destroy any plants or fruit that you suspect to have contracted disease.

- Ensure you are always clean. Virus or bacterium could be spread by your clothes, hand, and footwear. Wash your hands prior to and after working on your plants and wash your clothes as you might have been in contact with unhealthy plants.

- Clean your tools. Soil sticking to tools may accommodate disease organisms. Also, wash pots before you reuse them.

- Make use of clean containers and clean potting mix.

- Remove any already infected plants and those that have more than half of their leaves gone.

- Check for pest every day when you water. Remember to check on the beneath of leaves, because that the hiding place for starving bugs and their eggs.

- Decide on how much you are ready to deal with it. The plan is not to eliminate the pest, but to control it.

- Understand what pest you're having an issue with. Consult your local extension service if you are not sure of the pest. Doing this will make you adopt the pest control systems specific to your issue, instead of pouring varieties of chemical on the plant in an attempt to know which work better.

- Problems with smaller pests like whiteflies or aphids, spider mites, could be harder to control and might spread plant infections. To battle these pests, use organic pest control

- Build healthy soil which presents a friendly abode to insects and helps prevent numerous plant diseases.

- Plant at the right time, diseases and pests mostly respond to the climate, like the first warm day or the first rains. Consulting other farmers about these methods and observing the growth of each crop will assist you in knowing the best time to plant. Planting before the normal time will ensure crops are matured enough to resist diseases or pest that show up at a particular period. While planting, later on, could lead to the death of most diseases and pests due to no available food.

- Look for pests, observe if insects are helping or damaging your crops. Plant-eating insects are a usual part of farming. They do slight harm to crops as far as they strike balance with other insects, particularly the ones that consume pests.

- If you still experience pest attack after all the precautions, try (IPM) Integrated Pest Management

- If you need to act, make use of harmless pest control measures that are safe for your plants, you and the environment as a whole.

- Check up your crops frequently to help you know when to permit friendly insects to perform their duty, and the need to spray with natural pesticides or other pest control methods arise. When looking for diseases and pests, ask questions like:

1. Are the plants being eaten by an insect?

2. Are friendly insects keeping pest under control?

3. Is damage on the increase? Will it affect the crop yield?

4. Is it harmless, friend or pest?

At times the insects you easily see are defensive to your plants by eating the pests. And the plants might be at a growth stage where they could survive pest damage and stay healthy.

Worms are essential for healthy soil. Spiders, bees and most insects that reside in water are friends and help in controlling pests. As well, small wasps or flies with a long, thin tube at their back are friends. It is ideal is to leave a friendly insect to help your crops.

Pests damage crops by eating them or sucking the liquid in them

Sap-suckers includes mealybugs and scale insects, aphids, whiteflies, plants and leafhoppers, nematodes, mites and thrips

Plant-eating insects are snails, slugs, plant and pod borers and caterpillars

## HOW CAN YOU ELIMINATE PESTS?

Once you understand how pest destroys crops, you can make use of natural pesticides made for a particular pest.

Once you understand when pests show and how they relate to their surroundings, you can make use of physical techniques of pest control.

Spray with natural pesticides to prevent crops from being damaged and to prevent people and the environment from being harmed by chemical sprays. They are cheaper than chemicals and easy to make.

Natural pesticides often require proper care when used. Always remember to wash your hands after usage. Do not use more than needed. Ensure you always wash food prior to selling or eating them. If a type of natural pesticide doesn't work use another type, as they may not all work well in same conditions.

**Natural Pesticides for Plant-Eating Insects:**

Chili pepper, Garlic and pepper, dry and grind them to a powder.

Soak the powder (a handful of powder to a liter of water) in water all night.

- Pour the mix through a cloth to take out solids

- Combine a small amount of mild soap to assist pesticide glue to plants

- Spray the mixture directly on plants. Firstly examine your mix on one or two plants. If you observe that it's too strong, put more water and examine it until it looks perfect.

- Do same again as when due, and after it rains.

## Natural insect repellent for Sap-Sucker:

You can eliminate sap-sucker pests by covering them with oil that obstructs their breathing holes or mild soap. Mix mild soap and vegetable oil with water then spray the plants to kill the pests. Don't make use of strong soaps or detergents as they damage insects, soil, and most important plants.

## PHYSICAL METHODS OF CONTROLLING PEST

There are several physical methods of controlling pests or preventing parasites and predators, based on their life cycles and habits. Consult other farmers to learn more about the methods they use.

- **Animals And Insects**

84

Snake, frog, and a bird, observe these animals in your garden to know if they control the pest or not. Most of them consume pests and pollinate plants. With the kind of beak a bird has, you can notice what it eat by observing the way it acts in your garden. You can drive away crop-eating birds by hanging shiny paper, a scrap of metal and old cassette tapes near crops.

Nearly all bats eat mosquitoes. Some of them eat fruits while a small number of them bite animals. With thorough observation and by checking their leftover food, you will know whether they are eating insects or your fruits off the trees.

- **Plant a Variety of Crops Together**

Planting varieties of crops offer spaces for useful insects to reside and makes it difficult for pests to locate the plant they are fond of eating. Growing varieties of crops also increase food safety, if a crop fails, other crops will be available. The following are the reasons of planting varieties next to one another will guard against pests:

- Some flowers catch the attention of predators that eat pests

- Some strong smelling vegetables and herbs prevent pests

- You can combine crops with trees and animals to improve the advantage of each of them

- A few plants trap pests. Instead of eliminating pests, you can plant things that pests prefer to your crops. They will stick to the trap plants and stay away from your crops.

# CHAPTER NINE

## Harvesting Your Crops

Harvesting time varies with each crop. For you to understand the ideal time to harvest and the best means of picking to avoid damaging. The followings are a few things you need to know:

- Check the seed packs to understand the harvest time better.

- Check the number of days to maturity.

- If you are a new gardener, keep a record in a journal to help you make notes on your observations.

- Record what you have planted and the date to know the time they would be ready for harvesting. This will help a lot pending when you familiarized yourself with each variety.

As a gardener, you will learn gradually to be patient and not harvest before crops are ready. For example, pumpkins might look big enough to pick and eat, but they are not good to reap until the stem dries off, turned hard and vines die out. If you pick them earlier, the seeds might not be adequately matured to keep. The taste as well would not be at its best. Cut the stalks at about 5cm from the fruit to increase storage time. Let the pumpkins dry-off in the sun for one or two days to make their skin tough. They have a long storage life if they are well stored.

Another example is beans. They can be picked while they are young or give them more days to be matured before harvesting so that you can get the best nutritional value out of them

The maturity times of beans varied with the variety you grow. Variety like runner beans is as short as six weeks and could keep producing for about four months. Variety like bush beans and climbing start producing at about nine weeks provide you with abundant harvest for about three months. Zucchinis are ideally harvested young (approximately 10cm long if they are to be pickled) since they grow faster in hot weather and could suddenly turn into a marrow.

Plants use a vast amount of their energy in fruiting and flowering. Thus it is significant to ensure they acquire enough soil nutrients to assist them to produce plenty of crops, and also to build their immune system, making them more resistance to diseases and pests.

Bear in mind when harvesting crops like leafy greens, the best time to harvest them are late afternoon or early evening instead of morning to prevent eating avoidable nitrates in your food. The sunlight must have converted the nitrates in the daytime. Plants will discharge or share about thirty percent of the energy produced using photosynthesis in the day with the root area. This assists in feeding beneficial microbes that helpful to plant directly. While the microorganisms in turn discharge nutrients to the plants to keep growing.

# CHAPTER TEN

## Storing and Preserving Your Harvest

Storing your harvest is the best means of dealing with the surpluses of your crops against season when little is growing. The different ways to store your vegetables include freezing, drying and preserving. Some vegetables and fruits store well for months if you keep them in the appropriate conditions. What is most important is selecting unblemished variety and inspect them frequently, taking out any contaminated items. For instance, one spoiled pear can damage the entire bunch. Storing the harvests in a dehydrated, well-ventilated environment would prevent them from decaying. You can use a shallow cardboard box or wooden crate as well as storage boxes. Whichever you are using, ensure it gives room for proper ventilation.

Pears and apples are suitable for storing. Cover each fruit in paper and put in separately in the base of your container. Root vegetables like beets, potatoes, and carrots also suitable for storing. Remove the leafy edge of the carrots and beets put them in the box separately without covering. They both have the advantage of being covered by a layer of sand, making them tough. Potatoes could be stored in paper sack or hessian. Harvest them on a dry day and allow drying in sun. Take away any mire from the potatoes to stop from forming mold. Store them in a dark area to prevent from forming poisonous green patches on the outer layer. Leave parsnips in the ground over the winter and harvest when you need them.

Shallots, Garlic, and onions are to be dried completely and plaited prior to storing in a dry environment. The tops could also be removed and hang the bulbs in an old pair of netting or tights. Squash related plants like pumpkins can stay for about three months. It all depends on the type. Do not keep marrows and pumpkins after mid-winter. However, other squash like spaghetti and butternut can be kept till early spring. Make sure they are in perfect state and store them in a dry cool area like in the cabinet. A crop like zucchini doesn't stay long but can be refrigerated for about 3 weeks.

Leafy plants like spinach and lettuce don't store well, and they are ideal to be eaten in a few days of harvest. Plant more often in the early fall for you to have something to harvest in the cold periods. Legumes like beans and peas could be blanched and frozen or dried for use in a stew.

**Freezing your harvest**

Freezing is an easy and quick means to preserve your harvest. Freeze in usable sizes so the frozen crops can quickly defrost when using. Select only-ripe vegetables and fruits and freeze them immediately after harvesting. Put them in a plastic container or a sealed freezer bag to guarantee they are well kept and do not undergo freezer burn. Some vegetables and fruits will require blanching prior to freezing to prevent water in them rupturing and crystallizing their cell walls, leading to a soft consistency and boggy when defrosted. Just plunge the vegetable into a big bowl of boiling water at least ⅓ of the normal cooking time, and move to chilled water, before patting dry and freezing.

The following freeze perfectly well:

- Gooseberries

- Rhubarb

- Cranberries

- Peas

- Blanched beans (these include French and runner)

- Blanched apples

- Blueberries

- Raspberries

## Drying, pickling and bottling your harvest

Crops that dry better are apples, peppers, and tomatoes. Drying could considerably change the texture and taste of your crop and could make appealing additions to meals. Just clean and thinly cut your vegetables and fruits and place the pieces in a single layer on a baking tray. You usually leave it outside or sun to dry it out. You can use your oven to dry it, put your oven to its minimum temperature set and place the tray inside for some hours until pieces have dried up. Following that, store the pieces in a hygienic airtight container and eat within one or two weeks.

Shallots and beets are tasty after pickled and can be kept for some months. Clean and prepare beets  (do not take out the tops closer to the root, as it could lead to leaching out of color). Put in boiling water for about thirty minutes or until the heads and skins can be easily rubbed off. Cut them and put in a hygienic jar and wrap in pickling vinegar. For shallots, peel and trim the bottom and tops. Put them inside a shallow plate and wrap with salt to draw out surplus moisture. Leave them all night and clean carefully and put in a hygienic jar then wrap with pickling vinegar.

Made in the USA
Columbia, SC
14 March 2019